TANG KNIFE
with practical wire binding

KNIFEMAKING

FOR BEGINNERS

Stefan Steigerwald
and **Dirk Burmester**

4880 Lower Valley Road • Atglen, PA 19310

Originally published as *Messermachen für Anfänger* by Wieland Verlag GmbH, Germany © 2016 Wieland Verlag Translated from the German by Ingrid Elser and John Guess

Library of Congress Control Number: 2018958797

Photos: Peter Fronteddu
Cover design: Justin Watkinson

Layout: Matt Goodman
Type set in Minion & Frutiger.

ISBN: 978-0-7643-5734-3
Printed in China

Published by Schiffer Publishing, Ltd.
4880 Lower Valley Road
Atglen, PA 19310
Phone: (610) 593-1777; Fax: (610) 593-2002
E-mail: Info@schifferbooks.com
Web: www.schifferbooks.com

For our complete selection of fine books on this and related subjects, please visit our website at www.schifferbooks.com. You may also write for a free catalog.

Schiffer Publishing's titles are available at special discounts for bulk purchases for sales promotions or premiums. Special editions, including personalized covers, corporate imprints, and excerpts, can be created in large quantities for special needs. For more information, contact the publisher.

We are always looking for people to write books on new and related subjects. If you have an idea for a book, please contact us at proposals@schifferbooks.com.

CONTENTS

A FEW WORDS UP FRONT

Knifemaking is a wonderful hobby. More and more people have discovered how much joy it can be to create such a pretty yet practical utensil on their own.

The introduction to this enjoyable hobby is usually by means of a knife with a fixed blade. The two most common construction types of fixed blades are full tang knives and hidden tang knives. In the first case, the knife has a flat tang to which the handle scales are attached on both sides. In the other case the knife has a hidden tang with the handle slipped on.

In this volume, Dirk Burmester and Stefan Steigerwald show you both construction types. They make one knife each, following the individual construction principles, and lead you step by step with words and images through all phases of the knifemaking process. The steps are easy to understand and easy for anyone to follow.

You don't need any previous training and not a lot of sophisticated workshop equipment. A few simple tools and a suitable workplace are sufficient. You also don't have to spend a lot of money on materials—if at all. So actually there is nothing standing in the way of you starting your knifemaking hobby!

Through *MESSER MAGAZIN*'s workshop series, we want to help you with all technical questions and spare you quite a few errors. This series of books assembles a multitude of themes all around knifemaking in such a way as to enable you not only to follow each step but to do it yourself too. We emphasize especially the usability of all the volumes in workshop practice.

Thus all the volumes are provided with a wire binding. This way, the book stays open when you put it down. Also, we made sure that the size of the images and the fonts is big enough to still be recognizable and readable when the book is lying next to you during work.

We have tried to explain every work step in the most comprehensive way. But before you pick up your tools, you should read all the descriptions and explanations in this book. This way, you'll know what to expect and won't be confronted with unpleasant surprises later on.

I wish you much fun and success with your work!

Hans Joachim Wieland
Chief Editor, MESSER MAGAZIN

To create a blade yourself raises a lot of questions and comments. For example, "Is the steel hard already?" or "I have never worked with metal before." We hear this quite often in our little workshop. Thus, I enjoy it all the more whenever another person dares to tackle the subject.

I know the problems. When I started to make knives, there was not much literature available, and the internet, with all its forums, was not as sophisticated as it is today. So there is no lack of information. Sometimes there is even too much information, and the essentials are pushed into the background: taking one's time and enjoying the process, having patience, and being creative.

It is not as exhausting as you may think. And the reward is a knife you created completely yourself. Grab your drawing block and let's start!

—*Stefan Steigerwald*

Hidden tang and full tang knives? Didn't the authors cover this already? Do they do things twice now?

Yes, there are thematically similar books in this series. But we should start this topic from another perspective and enable easier access. For this reason, the knives in this book are exclusively made with tools available at every DIY store for minimal money. The only exceptions are a drill press and a preferably stable clamping device, such as a vise. Most hobby workshops have this equipment. And with respect to the drill press, you could borrow one from a neighbor.

The hurdles have never been lower before. Let yourself get infected with the knifemaking virus . . .

—*Dirk Burmester*

1. INITIAL CONSIDERATIONS

In General

Since we want to construct relatively simple knives with a fixed blade, no extensive considerations are necessary with respect to construction and technical realization. We focus on the basic work steps and working techniques that are relevant for all knives: clean edges, grind, finish, and so on.

At this point, the following tip for work safety can't be omitted: in order to show you the individual work steps in the most demonstrative way by means of photos, we partially had to abstain from safety measures that in practice have to be followed in every case. First, everybody who works with tools and creates shavings, abraded particles, or dust has to take care that the workpiece is supported in a safe and stable way. In addition, your eyes have to be protected by goggles. Dust created by working on handle materials can cause allergies (for example, working with exotic woods), or these materials can be poisonous (for example, mother-of-pearl dust can contain heavy metals), or they may be suspected to cause cancer (such as is the case when working with carbon). Thus, you should either wear a respirator or use a dust extraction system.

Basics about Knives

The hidden tang knife is a very simple construction: shaping the steel, putting the handle on—finished. At least in essence. Some important steps, such as hardening, were omitted in this description. The essentially simple and stable construction is the reason why many hunting and outdoors knives are built as hidden tang knives.

The full tang knife is not very complicated either: a piece of flat steel is shaped as a knife, then handle scales are mounted to the left and right. The full tang knife is a combination of various advantages. It is more stable compared to other construction types. Since the blade steel usually runs in its full width to the handle's butt, there are hardly any predetermined breaking points. And if a handle scale becomes loose, the tang still provides enough grip to work with the knife in an acceptable way.

A construction type that is even more stable is the integral knife, in which the blade, tang, and bolsters are made of one piece. But such a construction requires more machines and material and is considerably more elaborate. In addition, the full tang knife is distinctly lighter compared to an integral knife because of its less massive handle.

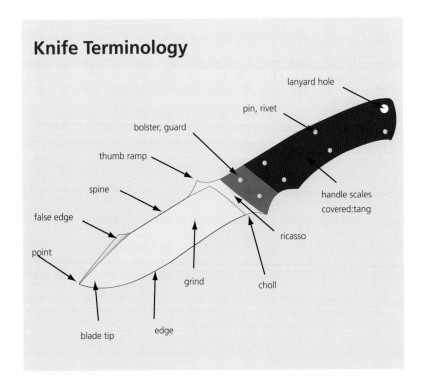

Knife Terminology

lanyard hole

pin, rivet

bolster, guard

thumb ramp

spine

handle scales
covered:tang

false edge

ricasso

point

grind   choll

blade tip   edge

But the disadvantages of full tang knife construction should not be concealed either: the larger amount of steel in the handle area moves the center of gravity toward the back, which means that full tang knives can be a bit handle-heavy if the blade is rather short. But the heaviness of the handle can be countered by drilling holes in the tang, or by a tapered tang construction where the tang tapers toward the handle's end. And although full tang knives have advantages in comparison with integral knives, they are still heavier than hidden tang knives.

If the full tang knife is neither made from stainless steel nor protected from corrosion by means of a coating, the tang may start to rust due to contact with sweaty hands, fluids, and—when used for hunting—blood ("sweat" in German hunter's jargon). But if the tang is completely surrounded by the handle material, such as is the case for a hidden tang knife, the risk of corrosion is lessened.

Which construction type you choose depends not only on the technical possibilities and the effort you want to put into it, but also on the intended use of the knife. Hidden tang knives have the lowest requirements with respect to construction. Full tang knives are a good compromise: they are stable and relatively easy to make. In addition, the construction allows many design possibilities for bolsters and guards that can be turned into reality depending on the knifemaker's experience, preferred way of working, and available tools and machines.

Our design for the full tang knife is a relatively small, all-purpose knife for everyday use. Because of their size, such knives are also called three-finger knives. At the same time, the design gives you the chance to develop your personal style. Our hidden tang knife is a bit larger and has the additional element of a guard worked into the handle.

Every user gives a different answer to the question of what size a knife ought to have. This also depends on the intended use. But blade lengths between 3 and 4 inches (8–10 centimeters) are sufficient for most uses and allow carrying the knife in public comfortably (and legally) because, in Germany, they don't fall under the prohibition of §42a of the German weapons law that prohibits carrying knives with a blade lengths of more than 4.7 inches (12 centimeters).

Blade Steel

Different criteria have to be taken into account when choosing a blade steel. It makes sense to start with a steel type that is easy to file and is available in suitable dimensions from knifemaking suppliers. It also should not be too resistant to our efforts with respect to the finish (grinding/polishing). In addition, we of course expect good cutting performance, which means the possibility to grind a fine blade edge, as well as good edge retention (long service life of the blade edge). To make maintenance easier, we decided on a type of stainless steel that is not too expensive.

We can't recommend using a piece of mild steel lying around somewhere, because it can't be hardened. It would be a real pity to put a lot of effort into a piece of steel that can't be used for the intended purpose, especially when a piece of sheet steel of proper quality is available at a very reasonable price.

When choosing the proper steel type, don't forget that you need a hardening shop to do the heat treatment. The shop should have experience with the steel in question in order to bring out its full potential and avoid warping. The suppliers of blade steel usually cooperate with suitable hardening shops and offer appropriate service. This way, many workpieces or entire loads can be pooled together, making hardening cheaper than placing an order at a hardening shop.

Our input requirements are thus specified. With respect to the choice of steel, many alternatives and many discussions exist. But an extensive discussion of the topic must be reserved for other volumes; for example, the benchmark book *Messerklingen und Stahl* by Roman Landes, published by Wieland Verlag. In addition, there is copious discussion around the issue online in the Messerforum (www.messerforum.net).

The choice of steel depends not only on personal preferences, but also on the intended use, the desired appearance, the possibilities for treatment, and—as always—on the price. In recent years the assortment of steels suitable for knifemakers has distinctly grown, starting with non-alloy or low-alloy carbon steels such as 1095, CK60, CK75, and 1.2842. These steel types provide fine blade edges, are able to be hardened, and are still sufficiently stable. Carbon steels can be heat treated, ground, and worked in a relatively easy way. In addition, they are cheap. Their disadvantage: they are not stainless (real "stainless" steels don't exist among "hardenable" steels—and thus among steels suitable for knives), and they tend to warp during hardening.

If the knife should be made of corrosion-resistant material, high-alloy steels (steels containing chromium) such as N690, ATS-34, 440C, 154-CM, AUS-8, or 12C27 are the best choice. These steel types have a chromium content of more than 12 percent within their matrix. The advantage of corrosion resistance is usually traded against a blade edge that can't be ground as finely as those made of carbon steel. In addition, with high-alloy steels there is a tendency toward lower elasticity. But this can be ignored for our blade length. The optimum hardness for use of high-alloy steels is a bit lower than that of carbon steels.

Various alloying elements such as chromium, vanadium, and molybdenum cause the creation of so-called carbides during steel production. Carbides are extremely hard carbon compounds that exist as small grains of microscopic size within the matrix and blade edge. Since the carbides are harder than the surrounding steel matrix, they generally enhance the edge retention of the blade. But if the carbides become too big, the matrix can't keep them and they break loose. Very small cutting angles in which the carbides stand relatively freely and are surrounded by little supporting material are less suitable for these steel types (recommended are included angles of about 40°).

To tackle the problem of too-large carbides, the process of powder-metallurgical (PM) steel production was developed. Common PM steels are CPM-S30V, S60V, RWL-34, ZDP-189, M390, and CPM-154. Steel types produced in this process create smaller and more evenly distributed carbides. Thus, elasticity and edge retention of PM steels are better than that of common chromium steel types.

The embedded, extremely hard carbides in general provide good edge retention for PM steel. But even for PM steels there is the danger that carbides will break loose from too fine a blade edge, depending on the included angle, material, and type of use (here we are talking about blade thicknesses in the realm of a few thousandths of a millimeter). Sometimes this trait is even wanted, because the resulting serration in the microscopic range is well suited for a drawing cut—for example, in hunting.

Another area is created by Damascus steels, in brief called Damascus. Because forging as a hobby and a profession has become more of a focus of interest in recent years, a large choice of forged Damascus is available today. Most Damascus steels are not resistant to corrosion. Exceptions are, for example, the stainless types of Damascus steel by Fritz Schneider and Markus Balbach. The Swedish company Damasteel also creates stainless Damascus steel in a PM process.

Due to the quality of modern mono steels, the use of Damascus steels is interesting only for optical reasons. There is hardly any gain in performance by fusing different steel types. For manually forged, high-performance Damascus steels, the degree of quality enhancement is not directly proportional to the effort and price. This does not speak against Damascus steel—individuality always has its price.

The items often neglected when discussing the right steel are heat treatment and blade edge geometry. These two parameters are as important for the cutting performance as is the choice of material. Only with a heat treatment matching the material and type of use does the steel achieve the desired qualities (hardness, flexibility, fineness of the blade edge, corrosion resistance). Insufficient heat treatment, in contrast, squanders the potential of the steel that is used.

The heat treatment of our blades is done in a hardening shop experienced in heat treatments of knife blades in general and with the steel types that are used. Since the blades are hardened in a vacuum furnace, almost no cinder (oxide layer) is created, which would have to be ground off afterward. This approach has the additional advantage that the blade can be ground almost completely while still unhardened, because prior to hardening, only 0.2 to 0.4 millimeters (mm) of the material has to be left.

The blade geometry has a decisive influence on cutting performance and robustness of the knife. The blade angle determines the force you need for cutting. The smaller the blade angle, the sharper the blade and the less pressure you need for cutting. On the other hand, the blade edge has to be matched to the steel and the intended use. Too fine a blade edge, for high-alloy steels, can lead to carbides breaking loose.

Knife blades are usually either hollow, flat, or spherically ground. With a hollow grind, the sides of the blade are curved inward; with a spherical grind, they are curved slightly outward. With a flat grind they are—as the name already implies—simply flat. By means of the hollow grind, relatively fine blade edges can be achieved even for thick blades. In addition, the blade achieves a classy look. But a hollow-ground blade with a very thin edge may get stuck in the material when it's being used for hacking. A blade more suitable for this with a spherical grind in turn is less suited for pressing cuts. Our knife will thus have a continuous flat grind. Here a flat grinding angle can be achieved that, in addition, is easy to sharpen.

Our demands are mostly met by the steel type Böhler N690. This steel is corrosion resistant, allows a sufficiently fine blade edge, is good to work with, and is also reasonably priced.

Usually the steel is hardened in a vacuum. As an "oil hardening steel" (a steel type that has to be quenched in oil for hardening), a blade of N690 after hardening has to be treated only with abrasive paper of grit 600 and can be finished subsequently.

Handle Material

For handle material, we decided on cow horn and masur birch for the hidden tang knife and French boxwood for the full tang knife. In general, the choice of material for the handle depends on your taste. Wood has the advantage of problem-free availability and can be processed easily. But it tends—like many other natural materials—to still be active after the completion of the workpiece.

Of course, optics is also important for the handle material. But nobody wants the laboriously created fitting to crack after a few hours of exposure to the dry air of a heater. Thus, the use of stabilized wood, soaked in artificial resin, is worth a thought or two. Alternatives are very hard and dense woods such as desert ironwood, African blackwood, boxwood, and ebony, which are not very active.

Stabilized woods have a surface feel that reminds one of plastic. This handle feel is not to everyone's liking. But if you use natural materials, you have to come to terms with the fact that, in the long run, volume and color hue change and, in the worst case, the material may crack or split. To counter these problems, you can mount slightly oversized handle scales.

When processing the handle material, you have to take possible health risks into account. The dust of many tropical woods is toxic or at least allergenic; the same is true for dust and fibers of compound materials. Stabilized woods contain acrylic resins, mother-of-pearl contains arsenic, and carbon fibers go for your lungs. Here, we repeat once again the safety tip we gave before: we urgently recommend the use of suitable respirators and dust extraction systems. The suppliers of materials for knifemaking will gladly help you with your choice of suitable materials or if you have questions about how to deal with these materials.

Tools

The topic of this book is the creation of a knife by simple means. The necessary tools in many cases are already present in a hobby workshop. If not, they can be obtained for minimal money in any DIY store:

- metal saw
- abrasive cloth and paper (abrasive cloth of grit 120, 180, 240, and 400; abrasive paper of grit 600 and perhaps 800)
- files and rasps
- dividers or scribing block
- round file
- metal drill
- shaped pieces for the clean grinding of curves
- clamping hand (or C-clamp, as an alternative)
- sturdy scissors (suitable for cutting cardboard)
- waterproof felt pen (white works well, but other colors are also suitable)

In addition, you need a stable clamping device, ideally a vise, and a drill press for some of the holes. While the clamping device is indispensable, you can also ask a neighbor or nearby craftsman for a drill press. It's only a matter of three drill holes!

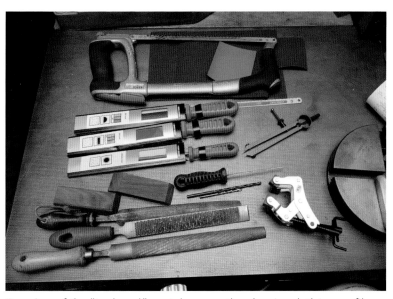

Overview of the "tool pool": metal saw on the abrasive cloth/paper, files, rasps, dividers, shaped pieces, drill bits, clamping hand. The files with the orange handles are low-cost items from the DIY store; the files and rasps on the bottom are part of our stock and are not absolutely necessary. But the round file with blue handle is quite helpful.

Clamping hands are useful, but not essential. You can save the expense.

As an alternative to the dividers depicted here, you can also use a so-called scribing block.

2. FULL TANG KNIFE

The Design

In general, a full tang knife gives you a lot of liberty with respect to design. We decided on a relatively small knife with a blade length of just less than 4 inches (10 centimeters) and a handle of about the same length. The nose on the blade is an additional design element and gives the design some more oomph.

When deciding on the ratio between blade and handle length, apart from aesthetic considerations, questions with respect to the intended use of the knife also come up. For a handy, all-around knife, other criteria than those for a kitchen knife, for example, are of importance. To answer these questions as well as those with respect to the effects of blade geometry on cutting performance, we point to the discussions in the German Messerforum (www.messerforum.net), for example, which are not always definitive, or to similar forums in English.

MATERIAL

Besides the tools described in the chapter "Initial Considerations," we need the following materials:

- sheet steel
- handle material (for this knife: French boxwood)
- two-component adhesive
- rivet material (rivet pins of round material or tubes)
- pencil, paper, cardboard, paper glue
- wood oil (for treating the handle wood)

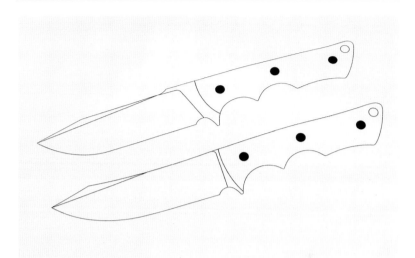

These two designs differ mainly with respect to the blade back (false edge, thumb ramp) and the ricasso's curve. To tell the truth: the finished knife, in the end, is almost exactly in between both, which means there is still potential left for our production tolerances.

The design is glued onto rigid cardboard and cut out carefully.

Special attention is given to the guard and finger grooves.

With the model, the fit to one's hand can be tested halfway realistically only when the finger grooves have been cut out accurately.

What we love on paper ought to rest comfortably in our hands later. Thus, we coarsely cut out our design and glue it onto a piece of rigid cardboard.

By cutting the cardboard meticulously along the lines of our design, we achieve a cardboard model that we can use to check the handiness. It is not a bad idea to toy around with the model for a while. If anything comes up that is not right with the "model knife," the design can be reworked accordingly and tested again.

It fits in this hand. Only when we are really satisfied with the fit to the hand—even when gripping the handle in different ways—do we turn toward the next work step.

Preparing the Blank

For our project, we used—for reasons already mentioned—the steel Böhler N690. Since the sheet steel is available in a practical thickness of 3.5 mm, we need to take off only a small amount of material.

We transfer the contour of the template onto the sheet steel by means of a scriber. If you don't have a scriber, you can of course use dividers. You ought to scribe especially carefully at the finger grooves, because they are responsible for making handling the knife as comfortable as handling the template.

It is ideal if the dimensions of the sheet steel are already close to the later knife: this saves material and, of course, also effort with taking it off.

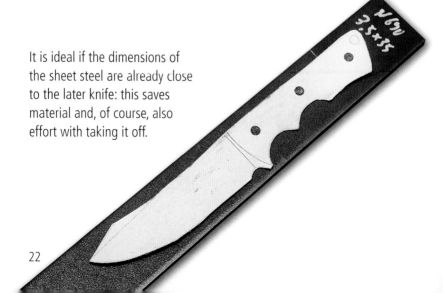

Here the contour is easily visible. By the way, the yellow digits constitute the material number issued by the steel institute VDEh, while "Böhler N690" is a trade name.

With a felt pen we draw lines onto the sheet steel, which are reference points for sawing the blank with the metal saw.

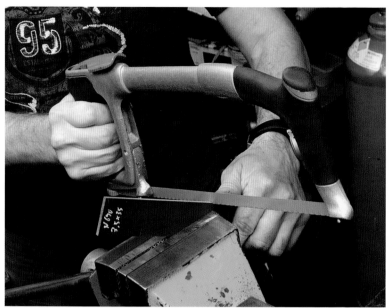

Careful sawing of the blank saves elbow grease when guiding the files later. The sheet steel is fastened in the vise and rechucked, if necessary. Now we can saw the blank along the white lines.

We can use the jaws of the vise as a guidance aid while sawing.

The blade's back is coarsely sawed. Here you can distinctly see that the jaws of the vise are used as guidance for the saw.

Since we stayed quite close to the contours of the actual blank, not much material has to be taken off after sawing is completed.

Working with Rasps and Files

Files are distinguished by their size, body shape, and cut and the shape of the embedded teeth. Rasps, in contrast to files, have separately cut teeth. If these teeth are hewed in or cut (negative rake angle), they act as scrapers. Milled teeth (positive rake angle) cut. Besides the profile of the teeth, files differ in the number and distribution of the teeth on the file body.

The term "file cut" describes the total number of teeth on the file that were created on the file body by stroking, cutting, or milling. In general: the harder the material, the smoother the file cut should be.

For softer material, also soft metal, files with cut 1 should be used. Their sufficiently wide distance between the teeth assures that no material gets stuck and clumps up on the file. For hard materials, files with cut 2 are used. On those, the so-called downcut has an angle of about 50°, whereas the upcut crosses at an angle of about 70°. The upcut creates the actual edge, while the crossing downcut (usually cut deeper into the file body than the upcut) ought to break off the shavings. Because of the angle, the teeth are set alternately, thus avoiding score marks on the material.

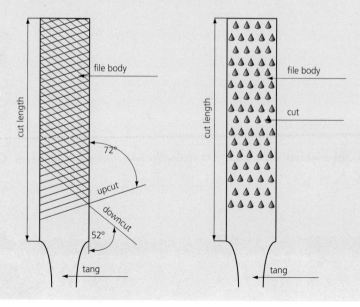

The cut number designates the number of notches per centimeter. The grade of cut is a means to distinguish between the various files. Common files have the grades 00 or 0 (coarse files for wood and soft materials), cut 1 (middle-cut files), and up to cuts 2, 3, and 4 (smooth-cut files). Very fine precision files have grades of cut up to 10.

Grades of Cut and Their Meaning

Depending on their length, files of the same cut have different cut numbers. The number of cuts per centimeter for Swiss-pattern files is approximately as follows:

GRADE OF CUT (SWISS-PATTERN)	CORRESPONDING TERM FOR AMERICAN-PATTERN FILES	CUT NUMBER
0	rough	4.5 – 10
1	middle	5.3 – 16
2	bastard	10 – 25
3	second cut	14 – 35
4	smooth	25 – 50
5	death smooth	40 – 71

Files are available in a wide variety of shapes: rectangular, triangular, round, diamond-shaped, semicircular, etc. For flat surfaces, flat or semicircular files usually are used. For working toward the ricasso, we use a round file. In this case it makes sense to use a file with a plain side to treat the blade surface, to avoid damaging the ricasso inadvertently.

There are other ways as well; for example, the transition toward the ricasso can be filed with a mill saw file, which is single cut at the rounded edges. So we achieve a rounded transition while working on a flat surface.

Files ought to be cleaned on a regular basis by means of a file brush. When the shavings are stuck between the teeth, the file acts as if it were blunt.

Shaping the Blank

Initially our blank is shaped with the file, then subsequently with abrasive cloth/paper.

Prior to dealing with the actual blade, we work on the blank's contour. First we use a medium-coarse flat file (cut 1) to shape the contour out of the straight line.

Then we use a semicircular file—also medium coarse—to work out the curvatures.

The closer we come to the final shape, the more careful we have to proceed so as not to botch the work (this means no grooves where they are not wanted, no exceeding the marked measurements, etc.).

The finger grooves are worked out carefully with the semicircular file. The file's radius ought to fit to the grooves; in any case, it must not be larger.

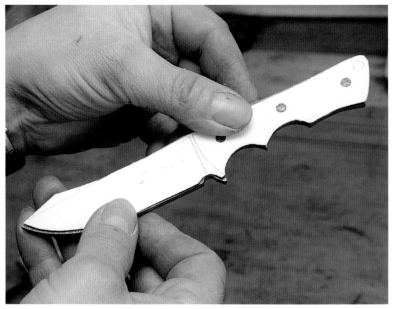

We regularly compare the blank with the template to prevent taking off too much material.

Here we still see some deviations from the model; for example, in the areas of the choil and guard.

To flesh out the choil, we chuck the blade into the vise at the intended angle.

Then we file down until we are flush with the vise.

The work at the choil, too, is checked regularly by means of the template.

For precision we use a fine round file with cut 2. Now we are about to start working with abrasive cloth/paper.

Working with Abrasive Cloth/Paper

As with tools in general, it pays off not to be stingy with respect to the quality of abrasive paper or abrasive cloth. With good abrasive paper and cloth you can work cleaner and longer. Abrasive paper and cloth differ in their carrier material. By its nature, abrasive cloth has a longer service life and is especially suitable with larger grit sizes. In addition, it doesn't clog up quickly.

A tip: abrasive paper should be kept separated according to grit (e.g., in a folder or similar place). This way you won't have any loose, coarse grains on finer abrasive paper creating deep grooves while working with it; these grooves would then have to be removed laboriously.

Flat surfaces should always be treated on a hard grinding base (wood, metal). This is especially the case for working on transitions, such as at the ricasso, where clean and clearly defined edges should be created. For grinding curved areas at the handle, we use abrasive cloth because the more flexible material fits better on shaped blocks and doesn't create unwanted edges. When grinding, each work step has to be completed before starting the next one. The finish with the grit that is used has to be perfect and regular. In addition, we change the direction of grinding with each change of grit size. Thus, grit for grit we grind at a 90° angle to the previous direction of sanding.

Differently shaped blocks for working on the contour.

In the area of the cutting edge, we omit working with the abrasive cloth of grit 240, because here we need to take off more material to shape the blade edge. There is an additional advantage to ending the work with abrasive cloth of grit 180 perpendicular to the blade's longitudinal axis: we still have to mark the central line with the scriber, which means that the contour of the blade edge is much more visible when it is at a 90° angle to the last grinding step.

First we grind the contour crosswise with abrasive cloth of grit 180, then lengthwise with abrasive cloth of grit 240.

When working on the blank with abrasive cloth/paper, differently shaped pieces are used as grinding blocks to achieve the desired inside radii at the handle. The piece of sheet metal here is only for pointing out the radius of the shaped piece, which otherwise is hard to catch with the camera.

Here we work with abrasive cloth of grit 180 crosswise with respect to the back of the knife blank. Thereafter we will work lengthwise with abrasive cloth of grit 240.

For shaping the finger grooves, we use round stock with a radius similar to that of the semicircular file with which we coarsely shaped the finger grooves.

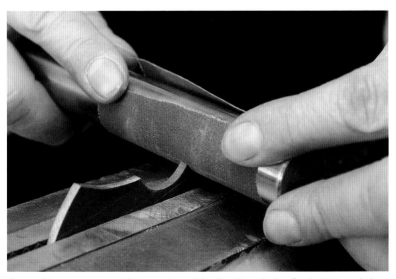

The radii too are ground crosswise with abrasive cloth of grit 180 and the round stock chosen before.

The abrasive cloth ought to be bent along the cloth structure in the carrier material or be folded to avoid tears and irregular gradients of the abrasive cloth, which otherwise can lead to an untidy result of your work.

Here the elaborate radii of the finger grooves with the grind lines across the material are distinctly visible.

The choil can be refined using the round file from before as round stock. To avoid blunting the round file, you can also use a suitable drill bit (here, 7.5 mm) as round stock.

When the contour of the blank is finished, we deburr all surfaces. For deburring we use abrasive cloth of grit 180 on a grinding block.

Now we compare the blank for the last time with our template and check its handiness. If no finishing work is necessary, we can now turn to the actual blade.

First we scribe the centerline of the blank (the position of the blade edge) with dividers.

The final grind on the side of the blade edge is done with abrasive cloth of grit 180 across the blank (while the rest of the contour was ground lengthwise with abrasive cloth of grit 240). Thus the scribed line is distinctly visible in the area of the blade edge.

We mark the position where the grind should end.

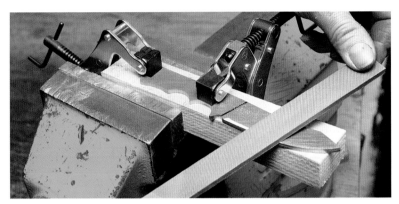

At first, a short grind is made on both sides in order to define the blade's center and thus the blade edge. In this photo, the blank is fixed with clamping hands. If these are not available, you first have to drill the rivet holes so the blank can be affixed by means of screws (see pages 40–41).

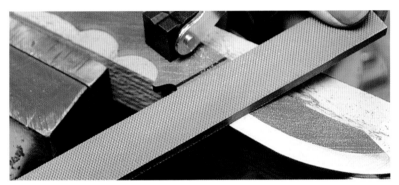

Now we make the grind up to about a third of the blade's height.

Important when working with files: pushing with pressure and pulling without pressure, so the shavings can break free from the cut.

We file crosswise to be better able to check the ground surface; if a uniform cross hatch is created, the area is plane.

When the short grind is finished on both sides of the blank, we transfer the position of the rivet holes onto the blank in order to prepare for the next work step.

We drill the three drill holes into the blank with a metal drill of the same diameter as the rivets (here, 4 mm). We can also use these drill holes to affix the blank with screws, in case no clamping hands are available.

The knife blank is held with two screws on a level surplus piece of wood, using the drill holes. Then the piece of wood can be chucked in without damaging the blank.

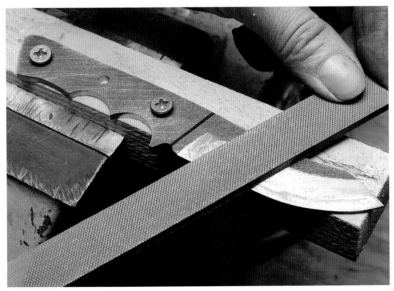

Now we take the grind up to the blade back while keeping some distance to the marked ricasso. Again we grind crosswise in order to better check the planeness of the created surface.

With the round file we now shape the ricasso.

Between the part shaped with the round file and the rest of the blade's grind, there is still a ridge. The scribed centerline marking the blade edge is easily visible too.

When removing the surplus material with a flat file, we have to be especially careful not to ruin the ricasso and blade surface we have just carefully fleshed out. As an alternative, we can work with the round file, slanted from above toward the ridge while keeping a sufficient distance to the surfaces, which should not be further changed in any way.

Subsequently, there follows the finish of the blade grind with abrasive cloth/paper. We start with abrasive cloth of grit 180. In case the grind still displays deeper striations, you can also use coarse abrasive cloth of lower grit size.

The ridge can be removed carefully with a flat file.

We grind across the blank with abrasive cloth of grit 180.

Afterward we grind lengthwise, this time with abrasive cloth of grit 240.

Now we shape the nose, which gives our design its special note. First we use a felt pen to mark the depth of the nose.

Now follows the already described process: we make a basic grind with the file . . .

. . . then continue with abrasive cloth of grit 180 crosswise and grit 240 lengthwise.

Then we work with abrasive cloth of grit 400 crosswise and finally with abrasive paper of grit 600 lengthwise. We put abrasive cloth 400 around a shaped block and work crosswise on the blank.

Again, our special attention is on the ricasso to avoid ruining the well-defined edge.

This image shows the same work on the other side of the blank.

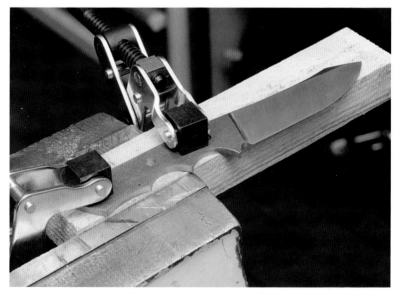

Intermediate result: to finish the transition toward the ricasso, we work from the ricasso toward the blade tip. Afterward we work on the blade along its longitudinal axis with abrasive paper of grit 600. The shine indicates whether the finish is uniform over the entire blade length.

With shaped piece and folded abrasive paper, we work from the ricasso toward the blade tip.

For the finish (abrasive paper of grit 600 lengthwise) we use a fresh piece of abrasive paper to avoid ruining the already quite smooth surface with shavings sticking to the used abrasive paper and causing striations.

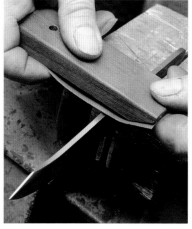

The contours are also treated further with abrasive paper of grit 600.

The result (prior to hardening) is worth looking at! Now the workpiece is getting hardened. Usually the vendor from whom you purchase the blade steel cooperates with a hardening shop. This approach has the advantage that the used steel is known, and normally no problems appear during hardening. The photo at the bottom shows the result after hardening.

The Handle

For full tang knives it makes sense to use a hardwood type (or another hard material) to achieve clean transitions toward the steel. In addition, hardwood is usually less active. Wood types with a density above 0.043 cubic inches (0.7 g/cm^3) are called hardwood.

We settled on a piece of French boxwood. With a density between 0.055 and 0.063 cubic inches (0.9–1.03 g/cm^3), it is probably the hardest European wood type, and in its land of origin, too, it is used quite often for knife handles.

The handle material will be riveted. We have already drilled the holes needed for this in order to secure the knife during filing.

The hardened blade, the handle wood, which is already split up, and the material for riveting (here, a small tube).

First we mark a drill hole (at the front or end) for the rivet material.

Now we drill the hole with a drill press.

 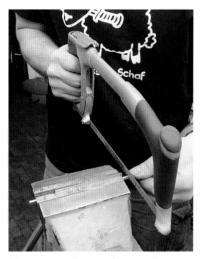

We saw the rivet to the appropriate length—two times the thickness of the handle wood plus blade thickness plus oversize.

Here we again use the metal hacksaw.

We deburr the rivet on a file that is not too coarse (cut 2 or 3). As an alternative, you can also use abrasive cloth of grit 180.

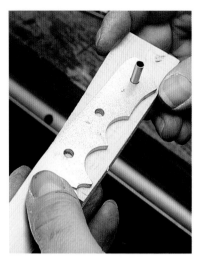

The blank is mounted onto the handle material with a rivet.

The second rivet hole is drilled through the blank. This way we prevent the drill bit from moving off-center, and no stress arises in the wood due to imprecisely guided drill bits.

It has to be possible to insert the pins easily: since drill holes in wood tend to shrink a bit, you can also use a special drill bit with a diameter of 4.1 mm instead of the 4 mm drill bit. If such a special bit is not available, we can also grind down the circumference of the rivet material somewhat by means of abrasive cloth.

In general, it is true that wood and other natural materials are active, thus creating stress in the material. For this reason, we should not provoke stress while working on the piece, because this may lead to ugly cracks even after just a short time.

Some wood types such as the popular snakewood are more prone to crack compared to other materials. If you are not sure, you ought to ask a material supplier you trust. They can surely give you advice and are usually able to offer you some pretty handle material at a reasonable price.

After the blank has been attached to the wood by means of the second rivet, we drill the remaining hole too, through the blank at exactly the right position.

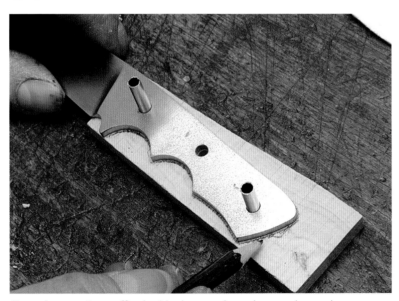

Since the two rivets affix the blank securely to the wooden scale, we can now draw the blank's contour precisely and without slipping onto the handle material.

The handle material derives from a piece that was cut in halves lengthwise. Thus, you have to take care to use the right piece for the right side of the blank. Otherwise there will be ugly disruptions in the imagined continuation of the wood grain across the blade's back, underside, or both.

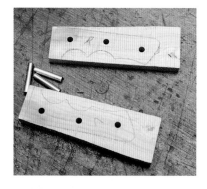

The scale is marked with *R* (*right*) so as to not mix things up later (right is the side of the blank that is on the right side with the blade tip pointing away from your body). The explained steps have to be repeated for the second handle scale (which, of course, is marked with *L* for left).

We draw the contour on the front side of the handle scale. The front side now has to be finished carefully and precisely because it can't be refined after mounting the handle material without the risk of scratches on the blade finish.

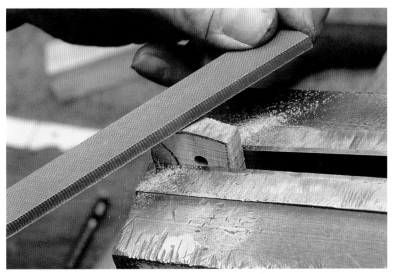

We file the front edge to shape. For this we use a file with cut 2 or 1. During filing, we have to be careful not to tear off any splinters from the wooden edge. Since some wood types are more prone to this than others, as a precaution you can use a leftover piece from sawing for testing. As an alternative you can file alongside the contour or use abrasive cloth of grit 180 instead of a file.

We check at the blank whether the filed curve is suitable and has a pleasing shape.

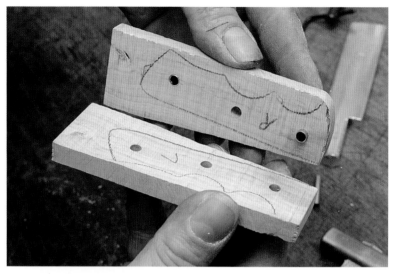

By means of the rivets, we fit the scales together.

The front edge of the first scale now serves as a template for working on the front edge of the second scale.

We now guide the file tilted to avoid tears. In addition, the front edge of the handle should be beveled—this enhances the handle's look and feel.

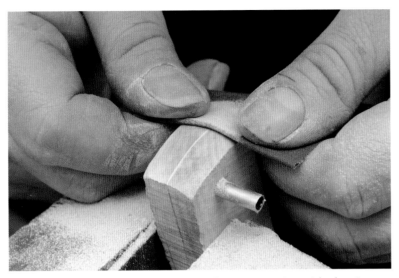

We treat the front end of the handle scales in succession with abrasive cloth of grit sizes 180, 240, and 400, then with abrasive paper of grit 600—lengthwise and across by turns.

When we are pleased with the result, we oil the front ends with our wood oil (see list of materials) to prevent adhesive from getting into the pores while gluing the handle scales to the knife blank.

We chuck the pair of handle scales and coarsely saw the contour with the hacksaw to ease the filing and grinding work done later.

The current status of work: all coarse work on the wood should be done as soon as possible to reduce already existing stress in the material or to remove stress created by processing before mounting (i.e., gluing) the handle scales. Especially in case the conditions during storage are unknown, it makes sense to let the just-treated wood rest for a day or longer and then check whether the wood is still plane. If you find deviations, you can still dress the pieces without problems.

The scales are ground plane on the contact surface facing the blank. For this we need a stable and level area and abrasive cloth of grit 180.

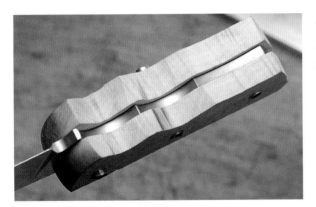

We check fit and look of the scales on the knife blank.

Since the handle scales ought to be glued on by means of two-component adhesive, the sides of the blank have to be cleaned carefully; for example, with cleaning solvent or spirit (look at the recommendations of the adhesive manufacturer). For oily woods, such as thuja or olive, the contact surface of the handle scales should be wiped off with a piece of cloth soaked in spirit to enable a secure bond.

The two-component adhesive is mixed in accordance with the manufacturer's instructions.

First we spread the two-component adhesive thinly and uniformly over the scales.

Now we treat the knife blank.

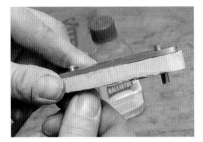

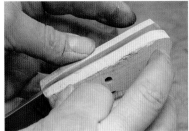

By means of the rivet, we can place the scale accurately on the blank.

We only have to put on the second scale.

The clamping hands (or C-clamps as an alternative) are screwed on only hand-tight to avoid the creation of stress in the material. Prior to further work steps, the glue ought to harden for at least twelve hours (here, too, stick to the recommendations of the glue's manufacturer).

Wrap the blade with kitchen paper, then with packing tape or something similar to protect the blade from possible damage during the further work steps. The kitchen paper, in turn, protects the blade from the corrosive effects of the tape.

In the following steps the handle material is adapted to the knife contour by means of the already used rasps, files, and round pieces. With the rasp, you ought to work at an angle toward the course of the wood grain in order to avoid chipping.

First we treat the top side with a flat rasp.

For the finger grooves on the underside, we use a semicircular rasp.

We slowly work toward the metal to reduce the danger of chipping. The material has to be left protruding a little bit because there are still rasp grooves in the wood that we have to remove later with abrasive cloth/paper.

An intermediate stage.

Here we can still see the different thicknesses of the handle scales, which are now to be matched.

At the same time, the rivets are shortened (also using the files). The rivets on both sides are filed flush to the wood.

To make the handle more comfortable for your hands, it should be contoured at its sides as well. For this we first mark the contour, which can be done using visual judgment. But the lines can also be transferred from an existing knife or be marked by using a roll of adhesive tape or another curved item.

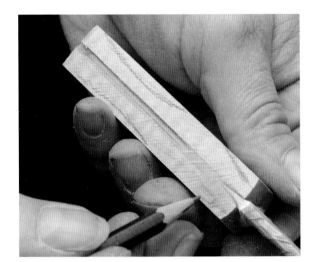

The contour is drawn first on one of the handle scales, then mirror-inverted on the second one.

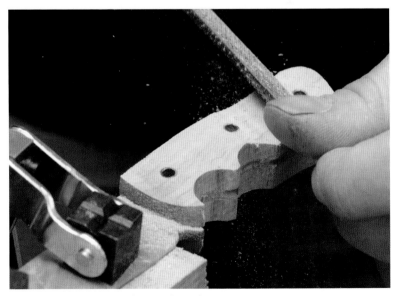

The contours are shaped coarsely with a rasp.

With a flat file we refine the area around the rivets.

The edges of the handle scales are beveled with a rasp: the first step toward a rounded profile.

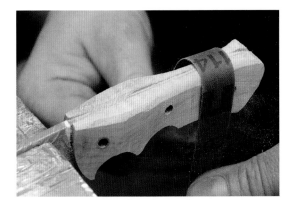

After coarsely shaping the contour with rasps and files, we continue with abrasive cloth. We start with abrasive cloth of grit 120 to preshape the contour.

If more material has to be taken off, this can be done with a fine file before using abrasive cloth of grit 240.

By pulling the flexible abrasive cloth across the handle, we automatically create the desired curves.

For refining the finger grooves, we again use the round stock we already used before.

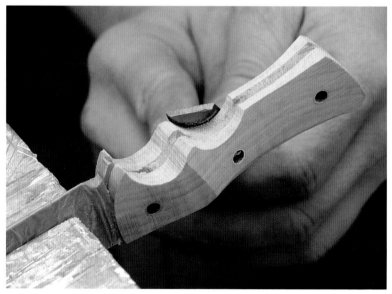

Now we bevel the edges at the finger grooves.

The "rechucking device" depicted in the following images, in which the knife is attached to a wooden block by means of clamping hands, allows quick rechucking of the knife in the vise. As an alternative you can use small C-clamps.

The following fine treatment of the surfaces is done by means of the grinding block with abrasive cloth of grit 240.

Here we have to take care not to grind away the contours we worked out before.

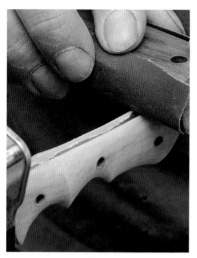 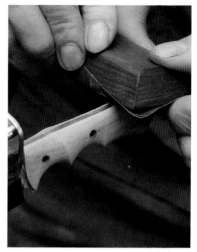

As soon as the glue on the blade back flakes off, we change to abrasive cloth of grit 400.

This way the blade back receives its concluding finish. The blade, in turn, is finally treated with abrasive paper of grit 600.

The well-known round stock is used again for the finger grooves—here at first with abrasive cloth of grit 240.

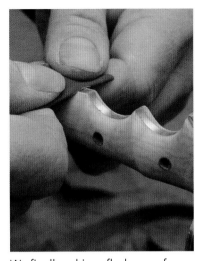

With abrasive cloth of grit 240, we work until we are close to the desired final state (wood and metal being flush).

We finally achieve flushness of handle material and metal with abrasive cloth of grit 400.

We treat the rivets with a reamer. This not only looks better but also prevents lint and other kinds of dirt from becoming attached.

If no reamer is available, you can also cut a small strip of abrasive cloth to size and use it as shown here.

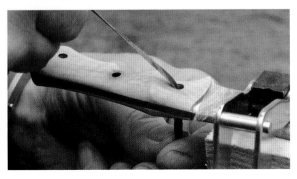

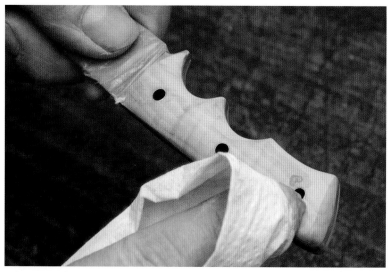

Subsequently we oil the handle with linseed oil or wood oil. The oil used for the handle ought to coat and solidify to make the handle more resistant to moisture and environmental influences. The drying time / air exposure time can be found in the manufacturer's recommendations.

To prevent damaging the knife handle, we wrap it with a soft cloth before chucking. The blade finish is done lengthwise with abrasive paper of grit 600. The knife looks even better after finishing it with abrasive paper of grit 800.

After removing adhesive tape and kitchen paper from the blade, we can sharpen the blade edge with a diamond file or by means of another method. In-depth information about sharpening knives can be found in the booklet *Easy Knife Sharpening* by Stefan Steigerwald and Peter Fronteddu.

The successful blade finish can easily be seen here: a satisfying result all around.

3. HIDDEN TANG KNIFE

The Design

We draw the design of our hidden tang knife on grid paper. The lengths of the handle (4.3 inches / 11.0 cm) and the blade (3.7 inches / 9.5 cm) were predetermined by us. Both values give the approximate proportions. The grid paper makes keeping the proportions and adjusting the design easier.

The radii of the curves can be drawn by means of a curve template, freehand, or by means of aids such as a roll of tape.

MATERIAL

Besides the tools described in the chapter "Initial Considerations," we need the following materials:
- sheet steel
- handle material (for this knife: cow horn and masur birch)
- two-component adhesive
- rivet material (rivet pins of round material or tubes)
- pencil, paper, cardboard, paper glue
- wood oil (for treating the handle wood)

What we like on paper should rest comfortably in our hands later. Thus we once again cut out a cardboard template to test whether the design fits our hands and doesn't pinch. The design is refined until the desired result is achieved. For this design we planned a guard (ferrule), which we want to make from cow horn, while the actual handle material is supposed to be masur birch.

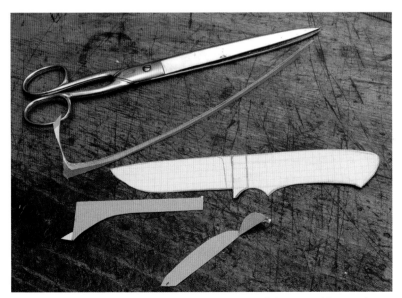

When cutting out the radii, we have to be as careful as possible to achieve a realistic look and feel.

Shaping the Blank

We have already cut the piece of steel to a size sufficient for our design. It doesn't have to be as long as the cardboard template, because we want to shape a hidden tang onto which the handle material is fitted. For a knife of these proportions, the hidden tang should have a length of at least 3.15 inches (8 cm) for sufficient stability. This means the sheet steel needs to be at least 6.9 inches (17.5 cm) in length.

The more stable (and thicker) the cardboard, the better you can judge how the knife will rest in your hand later.

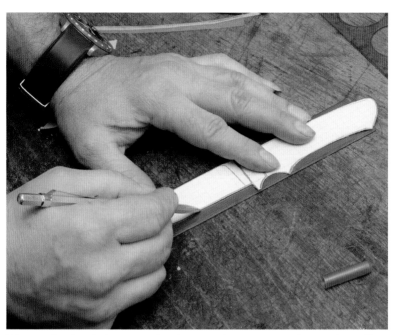

We transfer the design onto the sheet steel. Here we again use the scriber.

Now we draw the outline of the hidden tang on the rear part of the blank by means of a ruler.

The small width and conical contour of the tang reduce the amount of material needed and prevent the knife from being handle-heavy. As long as you don't overdo it and make the tang too small, you don't have to worry that its stability will be affected. In general, of course, it holds that the stability of the knife is enhanced with increasing width of the tang.

The tang can be placed centered but can also be a bit off-center toward the top or bottom. Ultimately this depends on the design of the knife: Is the blade supposed to protrude beyond the handle at the bottom? Do you want to work finger grooves into the handle?

To make the work easier, you can cut out the blank with a metal saw. This reduces the amount of material that has to be taken off with files. We already described this in detail in chapter 2 ("Full Tang Knife").

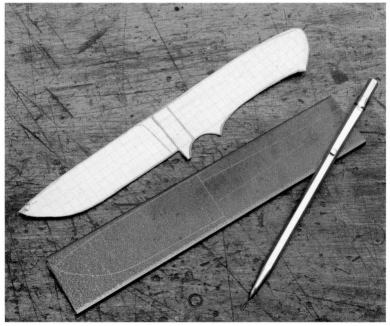

Here, we have already scribed the contour of blade and tang on the sheet steel.

Cardboard template, knife blank, cow horn, masur birch, and the two-component adhesive are at hand. We have already shown shaping the blank with the full tang knife. Here it is done in the same way by means of files and abrasive cloth/paper.

The blank is chucked with the blade facing downward in such a way that the scribed lines for the tang and the stop of the guard are flush with the vise jaws.

The stop for the guard is worked out with a file.

Here, too, the jaws of the vise act as a guide.

Now we break the edges on top of the blade because we want to provide the knife with an elegant blade curve.

For further treatment we place a piece of rubber between abrasive cloth and grinding block to achieve a gentle curve.

Subsequently we deburr the entire lateral surface of the blank with abrasive cloth of grit 180.

We mark the intended blade grind on the blank by transferring it from the template.

When chucking the blank along the markings, the vise jaws on both sides can be used as a "ruler."

We dye the side of the edge with a felt pen to enhance visibility of the scribed centerline.

When scribing, we work by flipping over from both sides in order to get two lines. These mark the material thickness that should be left prior to hardening.

We start to work out the blade's grind with a file.

This initial grind is made as uniformly as possible up to the blade tip. An illuminated magnifying glass makes checking easier, while at the same time protecting you from splinters.

This image shows the grind up to the blade tip and the safety margin toward the ricasso, which will be shaped later.

On the right side of the blade we work the same as on the left side until only the previously marked material thickness is left.

Our initial angle for grinding is rather steep.

The second grind follows. Here we create a second surface with a shallower angle. Felt pen markings quickly reveal whether we inadvertently take off material in the area of the blade edge.

Now we take the grind over the entire height of the blade.

We can clearly see the crosshatch pattern created by filing at a 90° angle to make it easier to detect bumpiness of the surface.

As with the full tang knife, we shape the area toward the ricasso with a round file.

Here there is still a lot of work left. But we have to work carefully not to cause any blemishes on the ricasso, which are hard to remove or to correct by changing the initial design.

Here, too, an illuminated magnifying glass supports working accurately.

By using a round file, a ridge is left over between ricasso and the rest of the blade. This ridge has to be removed later on.

This image shows the scribed mark for the blade edge. The ridge at the ricasso is still visible on the right side of the blade, while it has already been removed on the left side.

We remove the ridge with a round file. Of course, the surplus material can also be removed with a flat file. But it would be a pity if we blemished the ricasso or blade surface while doing so. With a round file, we can carefully work tilted from above against the ridge and still keep a sufficient distance from those surfaces that we don't want to change anymore.

An intermediate stage: the ridge has been filed flat on both sides; the transition toward the ricasso is nicely rounded.

As with the full tang knife, the blank is now further treated with abrasive cloth. We start with grit 120 and grind across with respect to the longitudinal axis of the blank. Suitably shaped blocks make clean work easier.

Now we work with abrasive cloth of grit 240 along the longitudinal axis.

Here we work cautiously from ricasso toward the blade tip in order not to damage the ricasso.

This is done on both sides of the blade until we have achieved uniform surfaces.

We cut a small strip of abrasive cloth to size and pull it across the blade's back. The strip should not be too broad, so the force on the blade acts as evenly as possible. In addition, we take care to work at a constant angle to achieve a uniform curve.

After using abrasive cloth of grit 400 crosswise, the finish is done with abrasive paper of grit 600 (lengthwise).

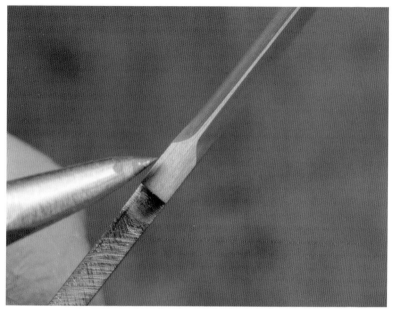

Again we check whether work on the blank toward the ricasso has been done evenly on both sides.

Our blank is finished and can now be brought to the hardening shop. The drill hole in the tang (diameter at least 2 mm) is used for hanging up the blade inside the hardening furnace.

The Handle

For our hidden tang knife, we want to combine a guard (a ferrule) of cow horn with handle material of masur birch. First we make the ferrule.

Our guard has no functional importance but is part of the knife's visual appearance. On the one hand it covers the blind hole into which the tang is inserted. On the other hand it makes the handle look livelier because of the color contrast to the masur birch.

We decided on cow horn because it is readily available, gives a nice contrast, and is easy to process. But you can also use other natural materials as well as plastics or metals. Of course, this increases the time and effort with respect to your work.

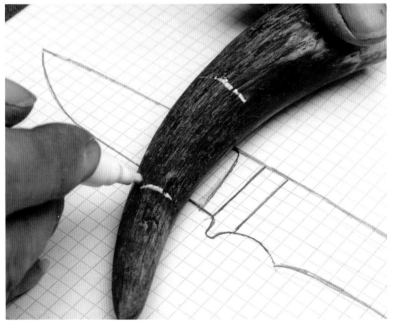

On a cow horn we mark a section of sufficient size for our guard. (Here our drawing of the cardboard template acts as a model.)

The marked part is cut out. The metal saw we used before is suitable for this work as well.

We flatten the cutout piece, at first with a rasp . . .

. . . then with abrasive cloth of grit 120, which we put onto a plane base.

Since we don't want to make bolsters, but a guard shaped like a ferrule, we mark the area where it is put onto the tang.

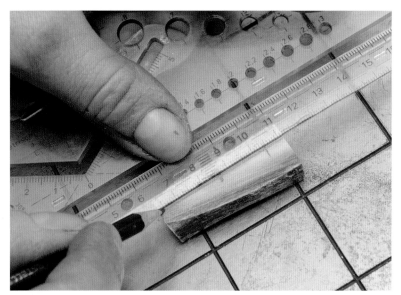

The centerline connects the beginning and end of the slot and serves as a mark for drilling.

To determine the suitable drill bit, we measure the tang's thickness. For the thickness of 3.53 mm measured here, a drill bit of diameter 2.5 mm or 3 mm is suitable. Thus there is still enough material left after drilling to shape the slot.

We drill the slot along the marked line.

The slot is straightened with a file on the top, on the bottom, and at the sides.

Intermediate state: the blade blank with prepared guard and handle material.

We check the guard's fit on the hardened blade. You ought to be able to put the guard on without much force, but the guard also has to fit without play.

Because we want to round the guard toward the blade, we draw the blade's outline as a mark.

We cautiously refine the surfaces of the guard until the fit is perfect. The bevel already hints at the later curvature of the guard.

As usual, after work with the file there follows work with abrasive cloth/
paper. We use a rubber base to round off the material.

While the right part of the guard is already distinctly beveled, on the left
side more material still has to be taken off to match it.

While working on the guard, we regularly check its fit on the knife blank.

We protect the blade with a bit of kitchen paper from getting scratched when chucking it in the vise.

The pipe for knocking the guard into place stems from the knifemaker's stock of material. As an alternative, for example, a washer with sufficient diameter can be put onto the tang, then a water pipe is put on top.

This hammer is a bit oversized. Here, the experienced knifemaker just grabbed the next best tool . . . Since the guard ought to be tapped into place only lightly, a hammer with a head of 200 grams is sufficient.

By tapping with the pipe, grooves are created. Here we have to rework the fit with a file. Checking the fit, tapping, and refinement are repeated until we are satisfied with the result.

Here, play is still distinctly visible between guard and blade. Thus more material has to be removed from the slot for the tang at the top and bottom.

With an angular sheet we check whether the fit of the handle material is at right angles with the hidden tang.

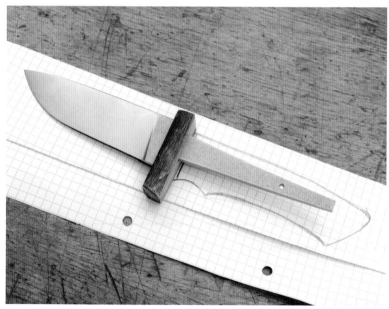

An intermediate state: we can refer to our drawing at any time in order to check whether the current result corresponds to our initial plans.

We transfer the outline of our hidden tang onto the handle material (i.e., the block of masur birch).

The extension to the front side of the block—after drawing the centerline—provides us with the points for placing the drill bit.

The drill bit for wood needs to be of sufficient length; its diameter matches the material thickness of the tang.

In accordance with the tang's angle, the block is chucked tilted. First we drill the lower hole . . .

. . . and then the upper one (but in general the order is up to you).

Now we remove the material left over in the center (please don't imitate this: using a round rasp is distinctly less dangerous).

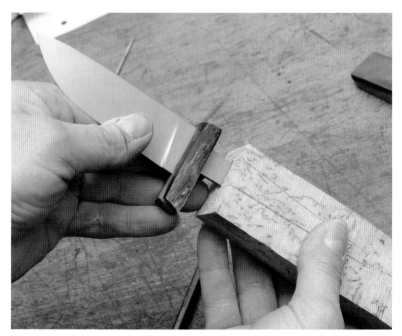

We check whether the hidden tang can be inserted completely into the drill hole. If this is not the case, we need to refine.

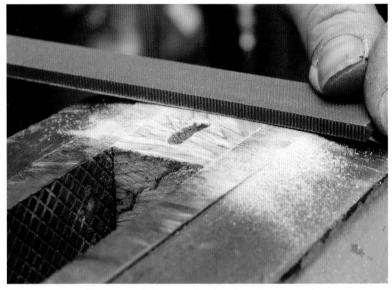

The contact surface toward the guard is first leveled with a file . . .

. . . and then with abrasive cloth, which we put on a plane base. The front end of the block of masur birch is treated with grit 120 and— at most—grit 180, because a bit of roughness enhances the glued bond.

We regularly check whether the guard rests neatly on the wooden block.

Now it is about time to mix the two-component adhesive. Here we ought to follow the manufacturer's instructions.

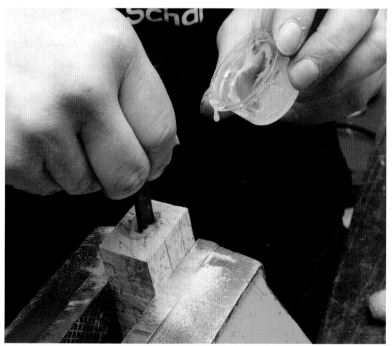

The hole for the tang is filled up to about two-thirds. We stuff the glue in with care to displace air bubbles from the lower part of the drill hole.

Two-component adhesive mixed to be highly fluid creates fewer air bubbles, but the hardening time is prolonged. We have to watch the processing time of the two-component adhesive to avoid setting before we have inserted the tang.

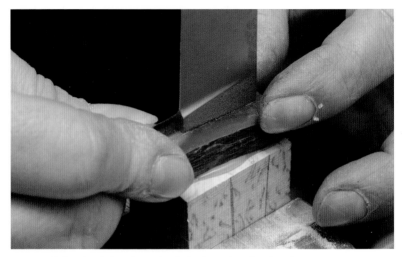

We carefully check for the right fit before the glue hardens.

Surplus glue emerging from the blind hole for the hidden tang has to be removed immediately.

Sometimes the blade "swims" a bit. This can be caused either by air bubbles still left in the glue or by material expansion while the glue was setting. Thus it is important to keep an eye on your workpiece while the glue is curing (usually about five minutes) and to carefully correct the tang's fit inside the handle material, if necessary.

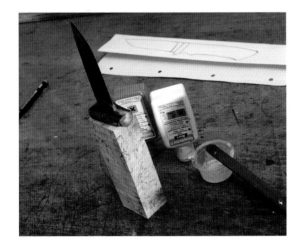

Prior to the following work steps, you should wait the amount of time for complete hardening recommended by the producer of the adhesive.

The current intermediate state: blade, guard, and handle piece are glued together.

We transfer the intended handle contour onto the handle material by means of our cardboard template.

The result looks like this, for example.

Again, we saw the contour coarsely with the hacksaw to make later work with files and abrasive cloth/paper easier.

If you want to saw along the handle, small lateral cuts are helpful to keep the saw blade from getting wedged.

Gradually we come closer to the final shape.

Now follow the work steps that we already described in detail before, at first with a flat rasp . . .

. . . and then with a semicircular rasp.

We draw the centerline as an auxiliary line for marking the handle contour on the underside . . .

. . . as well as on the top side of the handle piece.

Now we draw auxiliary points or lines, which ought to make shaping the handle contour easier.

We have drawn the contours freehand. Of course, using a curve template is also a possibility. Or you can use another knife that you have on hand as a handle model. Tape rolls or other round items can be used as well to draw the desired radii onto the handle.

We do the coarse work with the rasp.

The semicircular rasp eases shaping the rounded contours.

This work has to be repeated on the opposite handle side.

An intermediate state: the contour is coarse but worked out symmetrically.

Since there is still too much material left at the handle's end, we refine. Mounting the knife on a square piece of wood by means of clamping hands has the advantage that we can quickly rechuck the workpiece.

We draw a further auxiliary line running at a distance of a few millimeters parallel to the handle back.

With the rasp, we cautiously take off material until we reach the line, while making sure not to make the bevel too large.

On the handle's underside we use the rounded side of the semicircular file to better follow the contours. Don't forget: with rasps we work toward the material to avoid splinters.

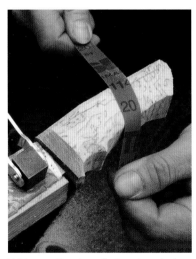

With small strips of abrasive cloth, we take off more material and approach the handle's final shape.

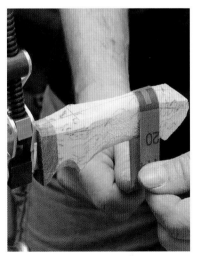

We round off the edged bevels created by the rasp so that the handle will rest comfortably in our hands later.

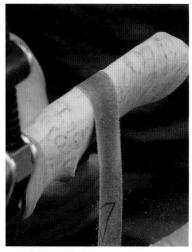

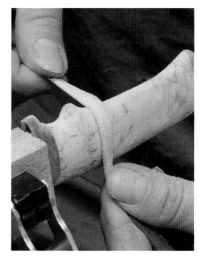

We continue the work with finer abrasive cloth.

The tighter the radii to be worked on, the smaller the strips have to be in order to achieve uniform results.

Now we are ready to use abrasive cloth of grit 400.

We work especially carefully at the edge of the guard because the cow horn can tear easily and we want to create a clearly defined edge.

Now we rub the linseed oil into the wood and let it solidify. As an alternative, you can use furniture wax, bees wax, etc. Cooking oil and similar oils are not suited because they don't solidify, darken strongly and can become rancid.

Before we chuck the knife again at the handle, we protect it with a soft cloth.

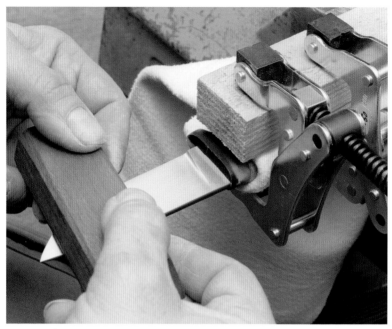

Now we finish the blade lengthwise with abrasive paper of grit 600.

Now the knife only needs to be sharpened. The image shows the use of the Wicked Edge sharpening machine.

Many methods exist for sharpening knives, from classic grinding stones to guided gadgets such as the Wicked Edge shown on the lower left, which ensures that the grinding angle is kept.

The method you choose depends on your abilities, preferences, and equipment. Some knifemakers swear by Japanese waterstones; others, by diamond files. It is important that the grinding angle is continuously kept and that you achieve a uniformly sharpened and really sharp blade edge.

After we have managed to make two totally different and very attractive knives, we can go on. The hobby of knifemaking provides almost limitless possibilities, up to very sophisticated working techniques and mechanically elaborate folding knives. Use the "Messer Magazin Workshop" series, which provides a lot of information and is a companion on your way to the ever-unattainable "perfect" knife. Have fun!

This knife, too, is quite impressive.

OTHER SCHIFFER BOOKS
BY THE AUTHOR

Pocketknife Making for Beginners
Stefan Steigerwald & Peter Fronteddu

ISBN 978-0-7643-3847-2

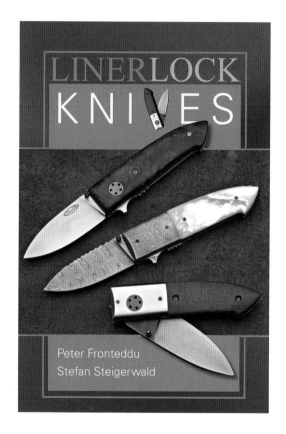

Liner Lock Knives
Peter Fronteddu and Stefan Steigerwald

ISBN 978-0-7643-5240-9

Making Full Tang Knives for Beginners
Stefan Steigerwald & Peter Fronteddu

ISBN 978-0-7643-4752-8